STOP PROCRASTINATING

HOW TO GET YOUR SH*T DONE

DR. MARYBETH CRANE

Table of Contents

Introduction:

Let me guess: You're the kind of person who sincerely wants to become more productive and disciplined, exercise regularly, eat healthy, wake up early, and finish tasks and projects on time.
But for whatever reason, you just can't seem to make these things happen. You struggle to follow through on your goals by successfully putting your intentions into practice. Paradoxically, you're unable to force yourself to do the very things you're sure you want to do.

Certain activities, for reasons you don't understand, feel too uncomfortable to pursue — indeed, you shudder just thinking about them. And so you end up wasting massive amounts of time watching TV, playing video games, dillydallying on social media, or otherwise distracting yourself. Then once you snap out of your distraction, you feel guilty about how you've spent the last couple of hours. You respond by harshly criticizing yourself, which further adds to your misery and causes you to drown yourself in even more distractions.

Does this sound anything like you? Good! You're in the right place. You're a procrastinator, and you're here because you're looking for a solution to end your struggles. You're here because procrastination is causing massive pain in your life, and you've about had enough. Maybe it's the constant guilt that's suffocating you. Maybe it's the building stress or anxiety. Maybe it's the relentless self-criticism. Or maybe it's the never-ending background feelings of misery, disappointment, and unhappiness that are weighing you down.

These sensations of shame, disappointment, and lack of fulfillment lead you to question whether you'll ever be truly happy, especially since you know deep inside that you're wasting your potential day in and day out.

I promise that if you follow the tactics outlined in this book, you'll immediately experience a significant decline in your day-to-day procrastination. You'll be able to start on tasks earlier, get things done on time, and feel a whole lot better about yourself in the process.

Will this book completely eliminate your tendency to procrastinate? Of course not. What you can expect, however, is to procrastinate a lot less.

Even better, you'll no longer feel so guilty about it, beat yourself up over it, or get super stressed about it. And as an additional bonus, you'll be able to enjoy your leisure time without constantly feeling like you should be working.

Sound fair? Let's get to it!

Chapter 1: How Procrastination Works and Why You Can't Stop

What exactly is procrastination, anyway? How does it work? Why do we do it?

The first question is the easiest to answer, so we won't spend a lot of time with it. Procrastination is the act of delaying or putting off something that should be done. The crucial ingredient in procrastination is that the delay is irrational. We know delaying a specific task isn't good for us, but we do it anyway.

The harder question to answer is why we do it. Why do we put off doing something that would obviously be in our best interest?

Why do we put off exercising when it's obviously good for us? Why do we delay studying when it's obviously what we should be doing? Why do we put off doing our taxes until we get multiple warnings and need to pay a fine?

This analogy may sound weird in the beginning, but bear with me. At the end of this chapter, it will all make sense and you'll hopefully be able to recognize your own behavior in what I'm describing here. And don't worry if you can't fully identify with the analogy or my overall explanation. The upcoming chapters will provide countless strategies that will work for you, whether you agree with my explanation or not.

With that being said, let's get after it.

According to our little analogy, the reason you procrastinate is because there's a monkey running the show in your brain. It's not a real monkey, of course. It's more like a second personality of yours — a personality that resembles the behavior of a monkey.

This monkey operates on the basic guiding principle: avoid what feels bad, approach what feels good. Its primary aim is to feel good right now and to maximize immediate gratification. The trouble occurs when what you (the rational part of you) want to do doesn't line up with what the monkey wants to do.

You want to study for an upcoming exam, meditate, exercise, or work on an important project. The monkey, however, has no interest in doing these things. None of them sound remotely fun or enjoyable. Heck, they sound boring, hard, and effortful — not exactly what a pleasure-seeking creature is looking for. And so, if you think about doing any of these hard things, the monkey starts revolting.

"Let's watch TV instead," it will say. "You can study tomorrow!" "Meditation is for monks. Don't kid yourself." "You'll feel more like doing it later." "Eat something first. You need some energy."

You're faced with a decision between what you want and what the monkey wants, between immediate gratification and long-term success. If you listen to the monkey, that's called procrastination. You put off doing what's best for you for something that feels better in the present.

If you don't listen to the monkey, that's an act of willpower. You use the strength of your will to veto the monkey. You forego the pleasures of the moment for potential benefits in the future.

 That's procrastination in a nutshell — a battle of impulse versus willpower, emotion versus reason, automatic versus controlled, experiential versus rational, and short-term pleasure versus long-term happiness. It's a battle between your rational self and your monkey self, between the part of you who wants to be healthy and the part of you who wants to eat candy all day long.

If you're a procrastinator, it simply means you're losing this battle too often. It means your monkey is in charge most of the time, guiding your behavior away from what feels bad and toward something that makes you feel good in the moment.

The good news is you'll learn exactly how to win this battle more often in this book. But first, let's dive a little deeper into how procrastination works.

When Emotions Get in Your Way

Procrastination has everything to do with emotions. Think about the last time you delayed something that you knew needed to get done. Did you experience any of the following thoughts running through your mind?

"I don't feel like it."
"I'll feel more like doing it tomorrow."
"I really don't want to do this right now."
"I'm just not in the right mood."

This resistance is coming from the monkey's desire to avoid what feels bad, and to avoid negative emotions. The tasks you procrastinate on always inspire negative feelings in you — dread, anxiety, frustration, boredom, and annoyance. Every time you experience negative feelings, the monkey shows up, urging you to mitigate these feelings. And what's an easy way to mitigate these feelings? Just put off the task.

Phew, what a relief! Now that you're not faced with the unpleasant task, you feel better. But for how long? This relief, as I'm sure you know, is usually short-lived. Sooner or later, any initial act of procrastination comes back to haunt you.

A great example of this is what I call the classic procrastination-guilt-procrastination loop. You don't feel like doing the thing you should be doing and, in the hope of improving your mood, decide to engage in something more fun. You check your email, scroll through your Facebook feed, maybe watch some YouTube videos. 30 minutes later, you realize you've been procrastinating for no good reason. Worse yet, you still don't feel like doing the thing. And on top of that, you feel guilty for having wasted so much time. Now you're experiencing even more negative emotions and your mood is even worse than it was in the beginning. This means you feel an even stronger urge to run away, making it ever more likely that you'll keep procrastinating.

In short, the initial act of procrastination leads to guilt (and other negative emotions like disappointment and shame), which leads to more procrastination, which makes you feel even worse, which leads to even more procrastination, and so on. Once you're in that loop, it's incredibly hard to get out.

Not only is the task you're trying to accomplish associated with negative emotions, but the initial act of delay piles even more negative emotions on top of those, making the monkey increasingly irritated. In that state, it's almost impossible to resist the monkey's pull away from the uncomfortable feelings and toward immediate gratification and short-term mood repair. That's another way of defining procrastination: as a short-term mood repair strategy. We can't handle our negative emotions and give in to feeling good. And while this works in the short-term, it makes things ten times worse in the long-term.

If we want any chance of overcoming procrastination, we need to get better at handling our emotions and impulses. Many strategies in this book will help you do so. Before we get to the actual strategies, however, there's one last thing I want to address…

Are Procrastinators Just Lazy?

In college, for example, some students could never get themselves to study until about two weeks before exams — they just couldn't stop procrastinating. It's this type of behavior that makes people think procrastinators are just lazy and careless when; in fact, the opposite is true: procrastinators care way too much.

Procrastinators, whether they are aware of it or not, are constantly worrying that:

…what they do isn't good enough
…people will "find out the truth" about them
…people will find out that they aren't as competent as believed
…they might get ridiculed
…they are inadequate
…and so on

Procrastination usually stems from some form of fear — fear of failure, fear of success, fear of the unknown, fear of judgment, fear of disapproval. It's much easier to procrastinate than it is to write a book and risk that people might not like it. It's much easier to procrastinate than it is to start a business and risk failing.

Whatever the exact patterns are, procrastinators tend to worry a lot. They experience more negative emotions when facing certain tasks than "normal" people. As a result, they also need more willpower and better emotion regulation skills than ordinary people do. Unfortunately, most procrastinators never learn any willpower or emotion regulation skills. The only coping mechanism most of us develop is procrastination: just put off the task; this will mitigate the negative feelings for a while.

After using this strategy for a while, procrastination becomes a habit. And habits are hard to break.
So, most procrastinators aren't lazy or careless. They have deep emotional issues that require strong willpower and well-developed emotion regulation skills — two things that the average procrastinator doesn't have.

Now, here's the thing: I don't know how to solve these emotional issues for you, and we're not going to dive deeper into these issues in this book. Instead, we're going to learn how to act and get things done in spite of those issues. I'm positive it'll work for you.

Let's get to it!

Chapter 2: Awareness

The first step toward any serious and lasting change is awareness.

Without awareness, change is at best luck-based or incidental. Think about it: If you're not aware of what's going wrong in your life, how are you going to fix it? If you don't realize how, when, where, and why you procrastinate, how are you going to prevent it?

Without awareness, you would not be reading this book. After all, you certainly wouldn't think that procrastination is a serious problem you need to be working on without awareness. So, kudos to you. You've identified that this is an area you should be working on. This is unlike most of your fellow procrastinators, who have no clue what's going on in their lives or they would take the necessary steps to fix it!

Even better, you took action toward fixing this issue by buying and reading this book. And who knows what else you've tried before?

The sad truth is that 99% of people out there will never even realize that they procrastinate, let alone take the necessary steps to overcome it.

You're already way ahead of the game. And if you keep reading and start implementing the strategies in this book, you'll slowly but surely weaken the impact procrastination has on your life. Along the way, you'll improve your productivity and become a healthier, happier, and more successful person.

A good way to illustrate the relationship between change and awareness is to consider a smoker who's trying to quit.

He needs to recognize that smoking is doing considerable harm to his health and make the conscious decision to quit. He needs to recognize the first sign of a craving and find a way to resist the temptation. He needs to see that if he gives in to the craving this time, he's more likely to smoke again next time. He needs to realize that he's most likely to smoke when he's drinking, and prepare his willpower beforehand.

The more awareness he has about his triggers for smoking, the better he'll fare. Without awareness, he'd have no chance whatsoever. He'd be running on complete autopilot, following the monkey's impulses and urges without even realizing it. He'd fail at all of his attempts to quit and keep smoking for the rest of his life without ever having a clue of what went wrong.

It's the same with procrastination. We need to be aware of what's going on.
Only then do we get the chance to change anything. If you don't realize that the act of procrastination will always lead to more procrastination in the future, you will keep running into trouble. If you don't see that you'll never "feel more like it tomorrow," you'll always rationalize your decision to delay. If you don't recognize that distractions are a major reason for your procrastination, you won't get rid of them.

The more awareness you have about the details of your procrastination, the better equipped you'll be to change. I would go as far as saying that the more recognition you have, the less you'll procrastinate. You see, awareness is oftentimes enough. Once we see what's going on, we almost automatically do the right things.

Now, here's the funny and challenging thing about awareness: We think we're good at it, but we're actually terrible at it. Most of our choices are made on complete autopilot, without awareness of our underlying motivations or future consequences.

In fact, research shows we often don't realize we're making a choice in the first place. Consider a study which asked people how many decisions related to food they made in a day. What would you say? The average guess was 14.

In reality, when the same study participants were told to carefully track their decisions, the average they came up with was a whopping 227 food-related decisions every day!

That's more than 200 daily decisions people were unaware of — and those are just choices related to food.

How can you improve something when you're not even aware that there is something to improve upon? When you're not aware of what's happening, your monkey is running the show and guiding your choices. You are following your urges and impulses without even knowing it.

The point is this: If you want to overcome procrastination, you need to increase your awareness of its many aspects. You need to pay a little more attention. You need to become a curious scientist — constantly watching, studying, and tweaking your own behavior.

The good news is that you'll automatically increase your awareness simply by reading this book and learning more about the topic of procrastination. Once you know some of the science and theory behind it, you'll start detecting patterns in your life. The mere act of identifying these patterns will help you facilitate change. (Yes, by merely reading this book, you'll get better at eliminating procrastination!)

More awareness is always a good thing, so I suggest using another strategy that will help raise awareness around your behavior and habits related to procrastination. It's called a procrastination log.

One of the best ways to increase your awareness of procrastination is to keep a log in which you track avoided activities, excuses, rationalizations, emotions, specific thoughts, and so on.

This record of your current behavior helps you see recurring patterns, learn from mistakes, and prepare better next time.

I suggest using a simple three-row spreadsheet with the rows "avoided activity," "explanation," and "plan."

Here are some examples you may recognize from your own life:

Avoided Activity
Explanation
Plan
Doing homework.

I was doing homework when Mike called and asked me to come over and try his new video game. I said yes and never got around to finishing my homework.

Next time I'm working on my homework, I'll put my phone on airplane mode.

Getting up early
I wanted to get up at 6 a.m. today, but I hit the snooze button and slept until 9 a.m.

Read the following implementation intention before going to bed: "As soon as the alarm clock goes off, I immediately get out of bed — no matter what!" If the problem persists, I'll create a commitment contract.

Exercise
I wanted to exercise after work today. Unfortunately I was a bit tired and told myself that it wasn't worth it if I don't have enough energy. That was, of course, just a lame excuse.

I can make exercising after work easier by preparing everything beforehand. From now on, I'll pack everything I need for exercising in the morning. I am also creating a plan: "When I get home from work, I immediately grab my training bag and head to the gym — no matter what."

Studying for an exam
I wanted to study on Saturday, but my friends urged me to go partying with them. I went, got completely hammered, woke up with a hangover, and couldn't get myself to study in that condition.

If my friends ask me to come party this weekend, I'll immediately answer in the following way, "Thanks, but no. I need to study."

Alternatively, I can still go partying but drink less. In that case, I can use the following implementation intention for myself: "After my first two beers, I will stop drinking for the rest of the night."

Paying the bills
For whatever reason, I just kept delaying paying the bills and now have to pay a fee.

From now on, I'll use the following plan: "Next time I get a bill, I immediately pay it."

These examples will hopefully give you a better understanding of awareness and why it's so important.

Chapter 3: The Paradox of Getting Started: Why the Problem Is the Cure

What do the tasks you procrastinate on tend to have in common? They all make you feel uncomfortable, anxious, or overwhelmed, don't they? Sometimes it's almost as if you're feeling actual pain when thinking about such tasks, right?

Well, that's because contemplating certain tasks does cause actual, physical pain. When researchers put people in MRI machines and ask them to think about doing a dreaded task, the pain regions of the participants' brains light up, signaling that they're experiencing tangible pain.

I'm not kidding. When you're thinking about doing the taxes, you feel actual pain. When you're thinking about exercising after work, you feel actual pain. When you're thinking about writing your dissertation, you feel actual pain. No wonder so many of us keep procrastinating! Nobody likes to feel pain (except for the occasional masochist, I suppose).

And what's our natural inclination when facing painful things? We shy away from them. Once burned, twice shy.

Of course we want to avoid and put off certain tasks — they literally hurt us. While some people can think about difficult tasks with no problems, procrastinators think about certain tasks and immediately start feeling bad. It's like I said in chapter one — procrastinators tend to have deep emotional scars that lead to having negative associations with certain tasks. It's not our fault that we feel this procrastination-causing pain, but it's our responsibility to learn how to handle it and function in spite of it.

Keep this in mind next time some smart-ass tells you something along the lines of, "Just do it already. What's the big deal?" Well, it's not that simple. And everyone who's ever struggled with procrastination knows that it's impossible to "just do it." That's exactly our problem — for whatever reason, we can't just do it. But I digress…

Coming back to experiencing pain when contemplating specific tasks, it may very well be that you're unaware of this pain in your day-to-day life. That's because it tends to happen unconsciously.

As an example, you may make the conscious plan to study after school today. At night, when going to bed, you may realize that you didn't do it. Whoops, what happened? Your unconscious mind steered you away from the pain, that's what happened. To bring back our little analogy, the monkey urged you to run away from what feels painful and toward what feels better. You may have watched some TV, had a nice dinner, and gone out for a glass of wine with your girlfriends — activities that feel good. That's the monkey unconsciously and automatically guiding your behavior away from pain and toward pleasure.

It will, of course, take a fair amount of awareness on your part to see these patterns operating in your own life.

And now for the good news.

Research shows that there's an easy way to get rid of the pain associated with certain tasks: Just. Get. Started. As soon as you start engaging in a task, the pain evaporates. Barbara Oakley, an expert on student procrastination, explains in her book, A Mind For Numbers:

"We procrastinate about things that make us feel uncomfortable. Medical imaging studies have shown that mathphobes, for example, appear to avoid math because even just thinking about it seems to hurt. The pain centers of their brains light up when they contemplate working on math. But there's something important to note. It was the anticipation that was painful. When the mathphobes actually did math, the pain disappeared."

Fascinating, right? The pain is in the anticipation, not in the actual performance of a dreaded task.

If you want relief from negative emotions caused by dreaded tasks, you can either procrastinate, which simply postpones the pain, or you can just get started on the task (easier said than done, but strategies are coming). Once you get started, the pain evaporates. And this near-instant pain relief isn't the only thing that's happening when we get started. Other research shows that the mere act of getting started powerfully shifts our perception of the task and ourselves.

Timothy A. Pychyl, a leading procrastination researcher, explains in his book, Solving The Procrastination Puzzle:

"Surprisingly, we found a change in the participants' perceptions of their tasks. On Monday, the dreaded, avoided task was perceived as very stressful, difficult, and unpleasant. On Thursday (or the wee hours of Friday morning), once they had actually engaged in the task they had avoided all week, their perceptions changed. The ratings of task stressfulness, difficulty, and unpleasantness decreased significantly… In fact, many participants made comments when we engaged them during their last-minute efforts that they wished they had started earlier — the task was actually interesting, and they thought they could do a better job with a little more time."

Once you get started, you realize it's not nearly as bad as you thought — the task isn't as daunting, unpleasant, painful, or stressful as you've imagined. Heck, it's actually kind of fun and interesting. And hey! You're not as lazy and unproductive as you thought. You can do this! You can be disciplined and get things done!

Better yet, you're now actively working on your task and are probably making great progress. Making progress feels great and so your mood, optimism, and self-confidence get another nice little boost. All of a sudden, you're feeling upbeat, positive, optimistic, and confident in yourself — you now have some powerful positive momentum on your side.

The small act of getting started creates ripple effects and sets in motion a whole machinery of self-perpetuating upward spirals. As you get started, pain goes away, perceptions change, and you start creating momentum. It's like Newton's law of inertia states: "An object at rest stays at rest and an object in motion stays in motion."

It's all about making that important switch from non-doing to doing. That's what procrastination comes down to: moving from non-doing to doing. A large part of overcoming procrastination means getting better at making that switch.

The good news is that you become better and better at making the switch every single time you do it.

Every time you overcome the motivational surface tension and move from non-doing to doing, you get better at it. Every time you manage to get started on difficult tasks, you build up that muscle of bursting through resistance and doing what needs to get done whether you feel like it or not.

Everything counts here. You either reinforce the pattern of needless delay, or the pattern of getting started and overcoming resistance.

Getting started is simultaneously the root of the problem and its solution. If you can't get yourself to begin a task, if you can't resist the pull of the monkey, you'll end up procrastinating. If you are able to get started, on the other hand, procrastination gets nipped in the bud.

To overcome procrastination, you need to get better at getting started, vetoing the monkey, overcoming resistance, handling negative emotions — call it whatever you want. Ultimately, most of the tactics in this book will help you with that in one way or another.

For now, let's look at four specific short-term strategies that you can start using immediately.

A major reason many of us procrastinate is because we're overwhelmed.

It's an uncomfortable feeling that is sure to get our monkey out of its cage. The monkey wants to run away from the uncomfortable feelings and, as a result, we become resistant to the task and experience an urge to do something more enjoyable. Because of that, we tend to be especially vulnerable to procrastination when facing big projects, which are naturally challenging and overwhelming. All those options, unknowns, and uncertainties are almost unbearable for the monkey, which is why it tends to run rampant when you're contemplating large projects. Where should you even start? What's the first priority? What's a reasonable deadline? What are all the things that still need to get done?

It's almost impossible to get started if all those overwhelming thoughts are swirling around your head. The key to overcoming this type of procrastination is to simplify things by breaking the project down into small, actionable steps.

First, create a list of all the things you'll need to get done. Second, create a plan — which tasks are you tackling first and in which order? Third, stop worrying about the steps further down the list and start focusing only on the very next step. Fourth, just get started on that very next step.

Stop worrying about getting it all done. Stop worrying about all the things left to do. Stop worrying about what's still to come — just keep focusing on the very next step.

Theodore Roosevelt once said: "I dream of men who take the next step instead of worrying about the next thousand steps."

And Mark Twain seemed to agree when he said, "The secret of getting ahead is getting started. The secret of getting started is breaking your complex overwhelming tasks into small manageable tasks, and then starting on the first one."

So, get in the habit of focusing on one thing only: the next actionable step. And then get started on that. Do not permit yourself to worry about the next thousand steps — that's a surefire way to get overwhelmed and procrastinate.

John Steinbeck, a Nobel Prize winning author, explains it perfectly: "When I face the desolate impossibility of writing 500 pages, a sick sense of failure falls on me and I know I can never do it. Then, gradually, I write one page and then another. One day's work is all I can permit myself to contemplate."

Don't allow yourself to look too far ahead. One small and actionable task is all you can allow yourself to contemplate.

Now, fair warning: This tactic isn't as easy as it may sound. It takes effort and willpower. You'll have to actively divert your focus from the overwhelming aspects of a project, then funnel it onto the next actionable step.

As long as you're able to keep your focus tight like that, your monkey will be humming along without disturbing you.

Invented by productivity expert David Allen, the two-minute rule states that if a task takes less than two minutes to complete, do it immediately.

Instead of answering simple yes or no emails "later," do so right after opening them. Instead of leaving the dishes in the sink for hours after cooking, wash them right after cooking or eating. Instead of bringing out the garbage "later," do it right when the garbage can is full. Instead of needlessly delaying paying your bills, pay them right after getting them in the mail.

Stop filling your mind or to-do list with an endless array of small tasks. Instead, get in the habit of ticking them off right when they appear.

Not only will this reduce how overwhelmed you are, free up a lot of mental space, and give you a small sense of accomplishment, but it will also get you in the habit of starting and finishing. Before you know it, getting started on small tasks becomes second nature. And sooner or later, that habit translates into the habit of getting started on bigger tasks and projects too.

Just following this simple rule helps you rewire your brain to get started on tasks, get more things done, and procrastinate less. Easy yet effective.

Implementation intentions are simple "if-then" plans designed to program your unconscious mind to act in a desired way in a specific future situation. For the "if" part, you pick a cue — e.g., a specific time, a thought, an emotion, or anything else — and for the "then" part, you pick a desired action.

"If situation X arises, then I will perform response Y."

If such and such happens, then I will do such and such. If I get home from work, then I'll cook a healthy dinner. If I feel the urge to procrastinate, then I'll ignore it. These plans sound simple and somewhat naïve, but they can be incredibly effective. They're sometimes referred to as "instant habits" because of their power to unconsciously guide our behavior in positive ways. We'll get more into the details in chapter five, which is solely focused on implementation intentions.

For now, let's form some implementation intentions designed to help you get started. Note that it's not necessary to use the specific if-then structure. As long as you link a cue with a behavior, you're good to go.

Here are a couple of ideas:

When I get home from work today, then I will immediately pack my gym bag and head to the gym to do my workout.

If I catch myself thinking "I'll feel more like it tomorrow," then I'll just get started on some aspect of the task.

If I feel too tired to do something, then I'll just ignore it and get started anyway.

Saturday morning after breakfast, I'll immediately start studying for my upcoming math exam.

After watching 30 minutes of TV, I'll immediately get started on writing my dissertation.

An outcome is always the result of a process. If you follow the right process long enough, you will eventually achieve the result as a natural by-product.

If you eat healthy, sleep well, and exercise regularly, then you will lose weight. If you write 1,000 words every day, then you will finish your book. If you play golf every day, then you will become more skilled at that sport. If you study for your exams for hours every day, then you will get good grades.

During your journey from where you are to where you want to go, you can either focus on the process or the outcome. If you're trying to lose weight, you can either step on the scale every day and measure your weight, or you can forget about the scale and just focus on making sure that you eat healthy every day. Likewise, if you're trying to build more muscle mass, you can focus on your weight and what you look like in the mirror, or you can trust the process and focus on eating well and going to the gym regularly.

When you're trying to get started on an unappealing, difficult, or otherwise uncomfortable task, it's best if you forget about the outcome and just focus on the process. It's usually the outcome that is associated with negative emotions, not the process. Writing a 500-page novel (the outcome) scares the crap out of anyone. Writing for 30 to 60 minutes every morning (the process) is a lot more appealing.

Next time you're trying to work on something you tend to procrastinate on, simply set a timer for 20 to 30 minutes. Tell yourself you're going to work on this thing for 20 to 30 minutes. That's it. It's that easy. It's nothing to be scared of. The hardest part of training for a marathon is the first 20 minutes of running!

Setting a timer helps you focus on the process and reduces a lot of the friction associated with getting started. You literally calm down your overactive brain and help it stop worrying about all the nonsense it tends to get caught up in. In other words, you stop scaring your monkey and soothe it instead (the negative emotions associated with the outcome tend to get it all excited).

You simplify things. You make it easy. And before you know it, you've started and good things ensue.

Chapter 4: How to Program Your Unconscious Mind to Automatically Procrastinate Less

Wouldn't it be great if you could program yourself to act in any way you like in the future? If you could just write a code for behavior and then automatically find yourself following that code? If you could plan today how you would act tomorrow?

Well, good news — you can do exactly that, with the use of implementation intentions, which we've briefly discussed in chapter two. As you may recall, implementation intentions are if-then plans that predetermine how you will act in a specific future situation. They look like this:

"If _____ happens, then I will do _____."

You are linking a cue (the "if" part) with a desired behavior (the "then" part).

"As soon as I wake up, I'll immediately get out of bed." "If I'm done eating, then I'll immediately wash all the dishes and clean the kitchen."

You decide now how you're going to act in the future. This allows you to make decisions from a place of calm and rationality. You get to ask yourself, "What would be the best way to act if such and such happens? What would I like to do if such and such happened? What would I like to do after finishing XYZ?"

Implementation intentions may sound too simplistic to be effective, but they're actually one of modern psychology's most studied and proven methods to positively change people's behavior.

In the remainder of this chapter, we'll discuss why implementation intentions work and look at some of the scientific proof of their effectiveness. At the end, you'll create your personal implementation intentions with the help of my examples.

It's fascinating what happens in our brains when we're forming these implementation intentions.

First, a link is being created between the cue and the desired behavior. If you wanted to go to the gym after coming home from work, you'd create the following plan: "As soon as I come home from work, I'll head to the gym." In this case, the cue "coming home from work" would be linked with the behavior "heading to the gym."

Next, the cue becomes heavily activated in your brain. This means that the cue is just dying to get noticed. It's kind of like the school kid raising its hand in excitement and trying to get the teacher's attention. Without any conscious effort or awareness of your own, your brain is now constantly scanning the environment in search of that cue (e.g., "coming home from work").

Once your brain detects the cue; the real magic starts happening. Because cue and behavior have already been linked, your brain automatically executes your predetermined plan. You'll find yourself packing your stuff and heading to the gym whether you're aware of it or not. Your unconscious mind simply takes over and executes your plan on your behalf.
Sometimes you realize what's happening and sometimes you don't. Either way, you'll find yourself doing the right thing. That's really the beauty and elegance of this intervention: that most of it happens below your level of conscious awareness. You can be busy doing other things while your brain is scanning the environment for you, detecting cues and guiding behavior — some people refer to implementation intentions as "instant habits" because of their automatic and unconscious nature.

And just like real habits, implementation intentions not only unconsciously and automatically guide your behavior; they also impact your willpower in desirable ways.

For starters, they conserve your willpower because you're not required to make conscious decisions when their habitual nature takes over. Preserving willpower means there will be more left in the tank to veto the monkey — to fight temptations and get done what needs to get done.

In addition to that, you're also able to better overcome bouts of low willpower. When you automatically do the right thing, it doesn't matter if your willpower is depleted or not.

So that's why implementation intentions work in theory. Now let's see the proof…

The Proof Is in the Pudding

Believe it or not, implementation intentions have been proven effective in changing people's behavior in over 100 studies.

They've been shown to help people lose weight, quit smoking, eat healthier, drive more carefully, and more.

One study asked students before Christmas break if they wanted to participate in an experiment of how people spend their holidays. Students who agreed were instructed to write an essay describing how they spent their Christmas, which had to be mailed in within two days of Christmas Eve. Half of the participants were given another instruction: to decide when and where they were going to write their essay. In other words, they were told to create an implementation intention.

The results speak for themselves. Two days after Christmas, 71% of students who predetermined when and where to write the essay had sent it in, compared to just 32% of students who didn't create implementation intentions. Think about that. Taking 30 seconds to create a simple if-then plan more than doubled the success rates of students.

Another study looked at tenth graders on summer break. They all had the goal of studying for their upcoming PSAT test in fall. In May, the researchers gave students a book with 10 PSAT practice tests and told them they would collect the book again in September when they returned to school. One group of students was also asked to decide when and where they would work on the practice problems over the summer months (e.g., "Monday through Thursday after breakfast in my room"). The students did not get a single reminder from the researchers over the summer.

After collecting the books from the students in September, the differences between the planners and non-planners was drastic. While non-planners completed an average of 100 problems, planners completed a staggering 250 problems. Again, performance more than doubled — all from one intention that took less than a few minutes to create.

Another experiment was designed to help people quit smoking through the use of implementation intentions. The results? Planners smoked significantly fewer cigarettes than non-planners over a period of two months. More importantly, 12% of planners quit smoking completely, as compared to only 2% of non-planners.

It doesn't matter what you're trying to accomplish; implementation intentions will increase your chances of succeeding significantly.

Heidi Grant Halvorson, an expert on the science of goal achievement, sums up the benefits of implementation intentions perfectly in her book, Succeed:

"Gollwitzer and his colleague Paschal Sheeran recently reviewed the results from ninety-four studies that measured the effects of if-then planning and found significantly higher rates of goal attainment for just about every goal you can think of: using public transportation more frequently, buying organic foods, helping others, driving more carefully, not drinking, not starting smoking, remembering to recycle, following through on New Year's resolutions, negotiating fairly, avoiding stereotypical and prejudicial thoughts, doing math problems… you name the goal, and these simple plan will help you reach it."

She adds: "Planning when, where, and how you will take the actions needed to reach your goal is probably the single most effective thing you can do to increase your chances of success."

Implementation intentions are an incredibly powerful and flexible tool to add to your arsenal.

Let's look at some practical applications for helping you win the procrastination battle.

Take a few minutes to think about your own procrastination habits.

What tasks do you tend to procrastinate on? When are you most prone to procrastinate? What activities would you like to engage in more often? What new habits would you like to build?

As you're thinking about procrastination in your own life, you'll realize there are lots of possibilities for using implementation intentions. Write down some if-then plans for your best ideas and repeat them out loud or in your head a couple of times. And don't worry about keeping your plans in the specific if-then formula. As long as you're linking a cue with a desired behavior, you're ready to rock it.

Below are some specific examples you can copy, modify, or use as inspiration. They are designed to help you overcome many procrastination-related problems such as not getting started, resisting temptations, overcoming times of low willpower, and so on.

If I feel overwhelmed by a large project, then I can break it down into small, actionable steps and get started on step one.

If I get bored during studying, then I'll ignore it and just keep going.

If I get discouraged during writing, then I'll ignore it and just keep going.

If I feel like hitting the snooze button, then I'll immediately get out of bed.

If I feel like delaying an important task, then I'll immediately get started on a small aspect of the task.

Saturday after breakfast, I'll start studying for my upcoming exam.

If I find myself making excuses such as "I'm too tired" or "I'll feel more like it tomorrow" or "I work better under pressure," then I'll just ignore them and get started on a small aspect of the task.

If I feel like watching TV, then I'll ignore it and keep working.

As soon as I get home after work, I'll immediately prepare a healthy dinner.

When it's time to go to bed, I'll write in my gratitude journal for five minutes.

Robin Sharma, a leadership coach and bestselling author, sums up modern world perfectly:

"We live in The Age of Dramatic Distraction. Many shiny toys to chase every waking moment yet so few of those pursuits create real value and grow a life brilliantly lived. Too many of us are overscheduled, overconnected and overstimulated by all the noise, interruptions and complexity of current society. The cost of this way of operating? You'll arrive at the last hour of your final day and realize you spent your highest potential on your lowest leverage activities."

The average American worker on an average day spends 2.1 hours in distraction, is interrupted every 11 minutes, watches 4.7 hours of TV, checks email every six minutes, and spends a total of 1.72 hours on email.

In the 1970s, 4-5% of people indicated that they considered themselves as procrastinators; today that number is at 20-25% — a five-fold increase over the span of a few decades.

What caused the epic rise in procrastination?

You guessed it — modern-day distractions such as Facebook, email, smartphones, video games, TV shows, and so on.

Piers Steel, a procrastination researcher and author of The Procrastination Equation, says this about the relationship between distractions and procrastination:

"…proximity to temptation is one of the deadliest determinants of procrastination. [And] the more enticing the distraction, the less work we do."

In this modern life, we procrastinate for as long as our work motivation is lower than our temptation motivation. Once the deadline is close enough, we become more motivated to work than to pursue a temptation — we stop procrastinating and start working.

More enticing temptations lead to more procrastination.

Modern life creates more and more temptations, while at the same time making them more and more attractive. Put another way; modern life creates more and more dashed lines while also moving them higher and higher. The solid bar, on the other hand, hasn't seen any changes over the last decades. The pleasure derived from work is still the same as in the recent past.

To sum up: Temptations become more attractive while work starts looking increasingly boring and dull compared to them. The result? Procrastination.

If we look at this relationship, it becomes obvious why we've seen such an epic rise in procrastination since the 1970s. Of course, people in the 1970s didn't procrastinate as much. What were they going to do with their time, anyway? There was no internet, no smartphones, no video games, no Gameboys, no iPod, no iPad, no Facebook, no Instagram, no Snapchat.

 Today, the internet alone is a candy land for procrastinators. In fact, it's now estimated that over 50% of time spent online is time spent procrastinating — the only technology-driven distraction people in the 1970s had was a TV.

And even then, it's not comparable to today. TVs in the 1970s didn't have 500 channels. They didn't have high definition. They didn't have the ability to record everything. They didn't have the ability to buy movies or TV series. They didn't have any features to skip forward or backward.

It's abundantly clear that modern-day, technology-driven distractions are a major enabler of procrastination. It's hard to meditate, exercise, read, or study when you could be watching TV, playing video games, or surfing the web. What do you think is more attractive to the monkey?

Oh, and the problem will only get worse.

The entertainment industry isn't exactly resting on their laurels. They keep refining their video games, online experiences, and TV features to make them more and more attractive and more and more addictive. And they're doing a great job at it — at the cost of your productivity and well-being!

If you want to even have a chance of overcoming procrastination and getting serious work done, you need to learn how to handle the allure of distractions.

In the remainder of this chapter, we'll look at three specific ways to do exactly that.

How often would you check Instagram if you could only access it on the roof of your house? Less often. But you don't need to go to your roof to access Instagram, Facebook, video games, TVs, etc., do you? The problem is most distractions are way too accessible — they're literally available to us in an instant.

Remember what we said earlier: Proximity to temptation is one of the deadliest determinants of procrastination. If we want to procrastinate less, we need to make distractions less readily accessible. We need to either completely eliminate a distraction, or complicate its access.

The good news is that's not hard to do at all. Here are some suggestions.

Block distracting websites. I'm talking about Facebook, Instagram, Snapchat, Gmail, news sites, and so on. You can block them on your laptop or computer using tools such as Cold Turkey. This tool allows you to schedule which websites you want to block and when. I personally find it very helpful. You can also block certain websites on your smartphone.

Delete distracting apps on your smartphone. I used to spend hours every day playing games, checking Facebook, or watching YouTube videos on my phone. Nowadays, distracting apps aren't even on my phone anymore — I just deleted them. It's radical, but it works.

Delete your computer games. If you're serious about overcoming your procrastination issues, any online or computer game has to go. (At least temporarily. Consider it a form of rehab with the possibility of re-introducing some games back into your life at a later point in time.)

Sell your Nintendo Wii, Xbox, PlayStation, etc. And if that's too much, at least put them somewhere you don't see them. (As you're about to learn in the next tactic, "out of sight, out of mind" is a good motto.)

While these strategies aren't bulletproof, they will at least make it a lot harder for you to give into temptations. Instead of opening your browser, typing "Fa," and entering Facebook, you now have to go into your website-disabling tool and somehow find a way to enable Facebook again.

The harder you make distractions to access, the less you'll procrastinate.

You've probably heard of priming before. It states that everything in our environment unconsciously triggers an action or behavior in us.

Sexy images can trigger the urge to have sex. The smell of cake can trigger feelings of hunger. Putting sweets on someone's desk in a clear, rather than opaque bowl increases snacking. Watching people being friendly can make us kinder and more altruistic.
Certain things in your environment can trigger the urge to procrastinate, while other things can trigger you to work on your goals and stop putting things off.

To procrastinate less, we need to mold our environment so that it triggers us to work more. Anything that could trigger our urge to procrastinate needs to go. Anything that could trigger the action of working is welcome and can stay.

Here are some ideas on how to incorporate this into your life.

Declutter your browser. Every visible hotlink or bookmark can trigger unwanted goals that distract you from doing what needs to get done. Your browser should be as empty as possible. No bookmark bar. No other visible bookmarks. No visible hotlinks. No website suggestions when you open a new tab. Your browser should not have any visible triggers at all.

Declutter your desktop. Same story. Quick launch icons and shortcuts can unconsciously trigger you to activate goals that are neither urgent nor essential. Your desktop should be as clean and simplistic as possible. For instance, my desktop is a nature wallpaper with one folder that I've creatively titled "Desktop."

Put that phone away. Turn it off completely, or at least put it in airplane mode (remember, the harder you make distractions to access, the less you'll procrastinate). And please put your phone out of sight somehow. If you see it from where you are working, you'll always be unconsciously primed to have a quick glance. No, it won't be "just a minute!"

Eliminate all notifications. Every notification on your phone, laptop, or computer can distract you and trigger the urge to procrastinate. Go into your settings and eliminate all notifications.

Take off your Apple Watch. It is the worst distraction while working. You can put it back on when you've reached your goals; even if you eliminate the notifications, it's still a significant distraction.

Declutter your work and living space. A disorganized, cluttered, and messy space is like a minefield of potential distractions and unconscious goal triggers. If you want to get work done, you can't have your Xbox, smartphone, gym bag, books, and magazines all screaming for your attention. To procrastinate less, radically declutter your work, and living space. Remove those triggers — out of sight, out of mind is the maxim.

Fill your environment with work triggers. What do you associate with your goals? What motivates you to get work done? What could unconsciously activate your goals? If you want to read a book at night, put it on your nightstand. If you want to write on a work project, put relevant material on your desk. If you want to feel more calm and mindful, put a small Buddha statue on your desk. If you want to feel inspired and motivated, fill your environment with images of some of your heroes. There are endless possibilities, and you can use anything as a trigger — quotes, Post-It notes, images, and so on. Set your environment with a goal board. It helps!

You can either create an environment that supports your goals, or one that entices you to procrastinate. Your choice.

Just like you can use commitment contracts to get your work done on time, you can use them to make distractions less appealing.

If you must pay $500 every time you play a video game, you'll stop playing it immediately. If you're serious about overcoming procrastination, this strategy can do wonders. Think about your worst temptations and create commitment contracts for them.

Let's take Facebook, for example. You could say that you allow yourself 15 minutes every day to spend on Facebook. Every additional minute costs you $10.

To set up a contract like that, you could do the following:

Download a tool called Rescue Time, which shows you your browsing activity.

Give a friend of yours, your spouse, or someone else you trust $100 or any other amount of money.

Tell your trusted partner that you'll only get your money back if you send them a screenshot of Rescue Time at the end of the week.

Tell them to keep $10 for every additional minute you spent on Facebook.

 It's by no means a perfect system, but it'll do the trick.

You can also use other third-party websites and tools to make this process easier. You can use Covenant Eyes (lets selected people see your website activities), stickk.com (the best website to create simple commitment contracts), SnuzNluz (makes you pay a certain amount of money every time you hit the snooze button), or Rescue Time (shows how you spend your PC time).

If distractions are a big issue for you, then I highly suggest setting up such contracts. Otherwise, you'll always find a way to rationalize your behavior. With a commitment contract, those rationalizations disappear immediately.

Chapter 6: The Willpower — Why It's the Secret to Overcoming Procrastination and Living a Successful Life

Procrastination can be defined as a form of willpower failure. We can also call it self-regulation failure, self-control failure, self-discipline failure, or whatever-else-people-call-it failure.

The issue is that you want to study more, finish projects on time, get up earlier, or exercise regularly. The desire is there, but you can't get yourself to make these things happen. In other words, you fail to regulate your behavior.

Procrastination shares this fate with many other self-regulation problems, such as excessive gambling, overeating, drinking too much, and reckless spending. The issue is always the same. The monkey is pulling you in all the wrong directions, but you lack the willpower to veto it.

More often than not, the reason we fail to regulate our behavior comes down to negative emotions. That's why the last chapter taught you a powerful skill to deal with negative emotions, helping you to better regulate your behavior in spite of them.

In this chapter, we're going to dive deeper into the science of self-regulation and willpower.

Since overcoming procrastination ultimately comes down to willpower — every time you resist the urge to procrastinate is an act of willpower — it is incredibly helpful to learn more about how it works and how to get better at it. Any improvement in your overall self-control directly translates into less procrastination.

The better you get at willpower, the less you'll struggle with procrastination. The good news is that willpower is very much subject to change. If you're willing to put in the necessary time and effort, you can strengthen your willpower significantly. In other words, you can become much more self-disciplined.

What can you do to improve your self-control? We'll get to that in a sec, but first, let's discuss some of the basics of willpower. Here's a quick Willpower 101 class.

What Exactly Is Willpower?

Over the years, people have defined willpower in many different ways. Some of the most common are:

"The ability to get done what needs to get done, whether you feel like it or not."

"The ability to delay gratification, resisting short-term temptations in order to meet long-term goals."

"Conscious, effortful regulation of the self by the self."

"The capacity to override an unwanted thought, feeling or impulse."

At its core, willpower is the skill of noticing what you are about to do and choosing to do the more difficult thing instead of the easiest. It's the skill of feeling the pull of the monkey toward immediate gratification and resisting it. It's the ability to resist short-term pleasure in favor of long-term success.

Why Is It So Important?

Willpower is the #1 predictor of happiness, health, wealth, and one's general "success" in life. Period.

According to Roy Baumeister, a leading researcher in this field, people with greater willpower are happier, healthier, and more satisfied in their relationships. They make more money and are further ahead in their careers. They are better able to manage stress, deal with conflict, and overcome adversity. They even live longer than their less disciplined peers.

Baumeister cites countless studies in his book, <u>Willpower</u>, showing that willpower is a better predictor of academic achievement than intelligence, a stronger determinant of effective leadership than charisma, and more important for marital satisfaction than empathy.

He sums up the benefits nicely in his book: "…found that improving willpower is the surest way to a better life.

They've come to realize that most major problems, personal and social, center on failure of self-control: compulsive spending and borrowing, impulsive violence, underachievement in school, procrastination at work, alcohol and drug abuse, unhealthy diet, lack of exercise, chronic anxiety, explosive anger. Poor self-control correlates with just about every kind of individual trauma: losing friends, being fired, getting divorced, winding up in prison."

Improving your willpower is the single greatest thing you can do to improve your life. And as far as procrastination goes, anything that enhances your willpower will also help you better deal with procrastination. The more willpower you have, the less you'll struggle with procrastination.

How Does It Work?

Psychologists often use the analogy of a muscle to explain how willpower works. Just like a muscle, self-control gets fatigued with heavy use, and thus varies in strength from moment to moment. Even the world's strongest biceps get tired sometimes, and so does your willpower muscle.

One classic study of this theory is called the radish experiment. Roy Baumeister and his team presented hungry college students with a bowl of chocolates and a bowl of radishes. Both bowls were placed in front of each student, who was then left alone sitting in front of the bowls. Half of the students were told to eat some of the chocolates and to not eat any of the radishes. The other half were asked to eat some of the radishes while avoiding the chocolates.

The researchers expected the radish-eaters to use up a significant amount of willpower. To find out if that was the case, the researchers gave each student a difficult — in fact, unsolvable — puzzle to solve. What interested the researchers was how long students would work on it before giving up.

Lo and behold, as the muscle theory would predict, the researchers found that the radish-eaters gave up much faster than the chocolate-eaters did. They had used up a lot of willpower resisting the chocolates and were left exhausted when trying to solve the puzzle.

This experiment has been replicated in different variations hundreds of times, and the results are always the same. If you've just finished doing something that requires a lot of willpower, you've spent a lot of your overall willpower strength as well. There's only so much willpower available in your tank. Once you've used it all up, you lose your ability to self-regulate on upcoming tasks.

You probably experience this in your life all the time. When you come home after a stressful day at work, what are you more likely to do: the easy thing or the hard thing? Watch TV or exercise?

With your willpower tank almost empty, it's pretty much impossible to veto the monkey's pull toward immediate gratification.

The radish and other experiments explain the first part of the muscle theory: willpower is like a muscle that gets fatigued with use. But there's another aspect to the analogy. While a muscle becomes exhausted by exercise in the short-term, it's strengthened by regular exercise in the long-term. Likewise, regularly exerting self-control improves your overall willpower strength.

One of the first studies demonstrating this idea asked volunteers to follow a two-week regimen to track their food intake, improve their posture, or track their moods. Compared to a control group, the participants who had exerted willpower by performing these small exercises were less vulnerable to self-control depletion in follow-up lab tests.

Another study showed that students assigned to a daily exercise regimen not only improved their physical fitness, but also became less likely to waste their money on impulse purchases and were more likely to wash the dishes instead of leaving them in the sink.

Roy Baumeister, one of the world's leading researchers in the field of self-control, explains it well in his book <u>Willpower</u>:

"Exercising self-control in one area seemed to improve all areas of life. They smoked fewer cigarettes and drank less alcohol. They kept their homes cleaner. They washed dishes instead of leaving them stacked in the sink, and did their laundry more often. They procrastinated less. They did their work and chores instead of watching television or hanging out with friends first. They ate less junk food, replacing their bad eating habits with healthier ones."

Over and over again, research shows that engaging in activities that require self-control helps build your overall self-control muscle. With all of that being said, let's discuss some of the best strategies to get better at self-control.

I purposefully use the term "get better at" because it's not only about strengthening your willpower; it's also about using it more wisely.

Oh, and be warned — strategies that are proven to grow your willpower muscle are, by definition, hard. You don't grow your biceps by lifting Styrofoam weights. Likewise, you don't grow your willpower by doing things that are easy.

If you want more self-control, you need to stretch beyond your current level — and that's hard!

Want to know the #1 reason people give for procrastinating?

According to Dr. Piers Steel, a leading procrastination researcher, it's fatigue. He writes in his book, <u>The Procrastination Equation</u>:

"Whether tiredness is drug-induced or not, being too tired is the number-one reason given for procrastinating; 28 percent of people claim, 'Didn't have enough energy to begin the task' as the cause… Fatigue increases task-aversion, saps interest, and makes the difficult excruciating."

The reason fatigue plays such a huge role is because the use of willpower, just like the use of any other muscle, takes energy. That's right. Every act of willpower requires and uses up energy.

If you resist eating a piece of cake, that takes energy. If you suppress an emotion, like anger or laughter, that takes energy. If you cook a healthy dinner in spite of not feeling like it, that takes energy.

Interestingly enough, the energetic component for the willpower muscle is the same as for any other muscle: blood sugar. Researchers have found that if people perform a self-control task (e.g., ignoring distractions or controlling emotions), their blood sugar levels tend to drop. And the more a person's blood sugar level drops after a self-control task, the worse he or she performs on the next task.

If you give willpower-drained individuals a glass of lemonade, the resulting boost in their blood sugar temporarily restores willpower.

Blood sugar problems (which translate into unstable and generally low energy levels) predict a wide range of willpower failures. Both diabetics and hypoglycemics are struggling to resist their impulses and delay gratification. All in all, people with hypoglycemia are more likely to be convicted of a wide range of offenses: shoplifting, public profanity, destruction of property, traffic violations, domestic violence, child abuse, and so on.

Low blood sugar levels translate into low energy. And low energy levels mean these people have trouble regulating their behavior, resulting in more crime and other self-control-related issues.

The same thing seems to happen with diabetics. (While they have high blood sugar levels, their bodies have trouble converting that blood sugar into energy, which also results in a lack of available energy.)

I've gotten a bit sidetracked here, but the point is that self-control requires energy. If you don't have energy, you don't have self-control. Or as Roy Baumeister puts it: no glucose, no willpower. It's that simple.

It doesn't even matter where your lack of energy is coming from — whether you've just had a tough day at work, eaten too much energy-draining junk food, consumed too much alcohol, have blood sugar issues, have adrenal issues, eaten too much food in general, or just have had a bad night's sleep. If you lack energy, you won't be able to withstand the monkey's constant pulls toward immediate gratification.

If you want to overcome procrastination, you need a good and stable supply of energy. In fact, I would go as far as saying that the more energy you have, the less you'll struggle with procrastination.

Let me repeat that: The more energy you have, the less you'll struggle with procrastination.

Anything you can do to improve your health and energy levels will help you overcome procrastination. There's another reason to eat healthy and mind your health!

The implications of this truth are rather obvious. If you're chronically sleep-deprived, stressed out, drinking too much alcohol, and stuffing yourself with junk food, you need to re-consider your lifestyle. If you're serious about overcoming procrastination, you need to get serious about your health and energy as well.

For starters, get enough sleep, optimize your diet, and exercise regularly.

In addition to that, I highly suggest investing some of your time and money into learning more about good sleep, proper nutrition, and exercise. I can tell you from my own experience that improving my sleep, nutrition, exercise, and other health-related aspects of my life has been absolutely game-changing for me.

Unfortunately, I don't have time to go into any specific health-related recommendations here. I can, however, point you in the right direction. If you wish to learn more about optimizing your health and energy levels, I suggest checking out my blog at www.fitfiftyandfabulous.com.

Making decisions is hard work. Depending on the type of decision, you must consider possible upsides and downsides, take responsibility, struggle with moral questions, and so on. It's an energy-intensive process that leads to a peculiar phenomenon called decision fatigue: The more decisions you make, the worse your judgment becomes.

Every decision you make takes energy. And unfortunately for you and me, that's the same energy we're using for willpower as well. Every decision you make sucks a little bit of fuel out of your willpower tank. The harder the decision, the more energy/willpower will be needed.

When you start your day, the tank is full (provided you've had a good night's sleep!). Every time you exert effort, you withdraw a bit of fuel, slowly emptying your tank. Choosing what to eat for breakfast drains a little bit. Same with deciding what to wear. Same with deciding whether to hit the gym before work or not.

Marketing experts have known about decision fatigue for years. That's why they put candy and other brightly packaged goodies at registers. As you make decisions while shopping, your blood sugar dips. By the time you're ready to check out, you're more likely to crave sugar to replenish your blood sugar stores than you were when you came in the door. The good news is you can reduce the number of decisions you make, helping you save your precious willpower to beat procrastination and put toward something else important to you.

Here are three simple things you can do to reduce decision fatigue and free up willpower.

Plan your day the night before. What clothes am I going to wear today? What should I eat for breakfast? Should I go running or sleep for another half hour? These are decisions that can be made the night before, which means you won't be wasting your self-control on those choices the next day.

Eat the same meals over and over again. I have the same breakfast almost every day — coffee and flaxseed granola with blueberries or oatmeal. For lunch, it's (almost) always a combination of soup and salad. For dinner, it's a decision between three or four meals I cycle through. Maybe a little boring, but it works for me. Very few decisions, right? Now compare that to the average person who's been shown to make 226 decisions about food per day.

Minimize your wardrobe. Steve Jobs was famous for his sneakers and black turtleneck. Barack Obama cycled through the same three or four suits during his presidency. Mark Zuckerberg has ten identical gray shirts in his closet. You don't need to go that far, but try to simplify your wardrobe a bit. I personally pretty much wear black. It all matches. The less stuff you've got in there, the fewer decisions your brain is forced to make.

As a general guideline, anything that helps you simplify your life will help reduce decision fatigue and keep more willpower in your tank to beat procrastination.

Exercise is one of the absolute best tools you can use to strengthen your willpower. Yes, you knew at some point I was going to go there!

Kelly McGonigal, the willpower expert I've mentioned, explains in, <u>The Willpower Instinct</u>:

"Exercise turns out to be the closest thing to a wonder drug that self-control scientists have discovered. For starters, the willpower benefits of exercise are immediate. Fifteen minutes on a treadmill reduces cravings, as seen when researchers try to tempt dieters with chocolate and smokers with cigarettes. The long-term effects of exercise are even more impressive. It not only relieves ordinary, everyday stress, but it's as powerful an antidepressant as Prozac. Working out also enhances the biology of self-control by increasing baseline heart rate variability and training the brain. When neuroscientists have peered inside the brains of new exercisers, they have seen increases in both gray matter — brain cells — and white matter, the insulation on brain cells that helps them communicate quickly and efficiently with each other. Physical exercise — like meditation — makes your brain bigger and faster, and the prefrontal cortex shows the largest training effect."

The immediate question this quote provokes is: How much do I need to do?

The right answer depends on how much you're willing to do. Setting unrealistic goals that you're going to abandon in a week makes no sense. Besides that, there's no scientific consensus about how much exercise you need to do. It's best to start with a modest and realistic goal — consistency over intensity is the maxim.

Anything that you like to do and gets you moving is great. Best of all, walking, running, biking, gardening, grocery shopping, yoga, swimming, dancing, playing with your kids or pets — they all count!

Self-compassion is another great way to boost self-control.

 Here's a short and concise explanation from Kelly McGonigal in <u>The Willpower Instinct</u>:

"If you think that the key to greater willpower is being harder on yourself, you are not alone. But you are wrong. Study after study shows that self-criticism is consistently associated with less motivation and worse self-control. It is also one of the single biggest predictors of depression, which drains both "I will" power and "I want" power. In contrast, self-compassion — being supportive and kind to yourself, especially in the face of stress and failure — is associated with more motivation and better self-control."

The more self-critical participants were in response to procrastinating the first time, the longer they procrastinated for the next exam. It's forgiveness, not guilt, which maximizes self-control and performance.

Self-compassionate has made a substantial difference in my life. Not only does it help me procrastinate less, but it makes me happier, healthier, and more successful in general. Ultimately, it comes down to the question of how you want to coach yourself.

Think about it. If you could pick a coach who follows you 24/7 for the rest of your life, who would you pick?

The guy who criticizes you all the time, puts you down, makes you small, beats you up mentally, punishes you, and rules with a demoralizing whip? Or the guy who looks out for you, cares for you, treats you with respect, has your best interests in mind, picks you up when you're feeling down, and motivates you?

If you want to be a good coach for yourself and overcome procrastination along the way, leave self-criticism behind and choose the path of self-compassion.

The good news is, no matter how self-critical you currently are, you can change it. Self-compassion, just like willpower, is a muscle. The more you train it, the better you get at it.

The best way to grow your self-compassion muscle is simply to use it regularly. Every time you're not feeling so well is a chance to practice compassion for yourself — maybe you're feeling angry, lonely, depressed, sad, or disappointed. In such a moment of suffering, treat yourself like you would treat a good friend: with love, warmth, and care.

Realize it's okay to feel this way and that other people feel this way too. It's normal to be imperfect and struggle from time to time. Realize also that any thoughts and emotions are impermanent; they come and go like clouds in the sky. See if you can simply watch your inner world as a compassionate, nonjudgmental observer. You can even try to console and comfort yourself by talking to yourself in a kind, sympathetic, and understanding way. If you feel like it, you can give yourself a hug, gently stroke your arms, or lay your hands on your heart. I know it sounds a bit silly at first, but give it a try.

What have you got to lose? It's not like other people are watching — they're too busy struggling with their own issues! And if you want to learn more about the science of self-compassion, check out Kristin Neff's similarly titled book.

Above All, Practice, Practice, Practice

Self-control is a skill like any other. If you want to get better at it, you need to practice.

You see, the secret to superhuman willpower is willpower itself: self-discipline begets self-discipline. Every time you act with discipline, you grow that muscle and become a little bit more disciplined.

Every time you resist the cookie, you grow your willpower. Every time you opt for a book instead of the TV, you grow your willpower. Every time you resist the urge to check Facebook, you grow your willpower. Every time you get up early and resist hitting the snooze button, you grow your willpower. Every time you prioritize sleep over watching another episode of your favorite TV show, you grow your willpower. And remember, growing your willpower muscle directly translates into procrastinating less.

Before we wrap up this chapter, there are two things I would like you to keep in mind on your journey to having more self-control.

First of all, start small. Don't try to go from zero to hero. Don't aim to get up early, go for a morning run, take a cold shower, and then meditate for 20 minutes. Unless you're already very disciplined, this is a recipe for failure, discouragement, and self-criticism. Instead, start small. Slowly cut back on negative habits. Slowly build your life around positive, willpower-supporting habits. If you do that, you'll find your self-control steadily becoming stronger and stronger.

Second, expect lots of setbacks and drama on your journey. You'll inevitably experience periods of despair, disappointment, and discouragement. You'll feel like nothing's working and you're moving backwards instead of forwards. You'll start doubting yourself. You'll fall back into old habits. And so on and so forth. That's to be expected. The best thing you can do during those times is to work on your self-compassion.

Above all, stay patient — building self-control takes time. Just keep at it and you'll be sure to reap the rewards.

Conclusion:

Well, there you have it.

Congrats on making it all the way to the end of this book. For a (soon to be ex-) procrastinator, that's a monumental task.

Hopefully, you've had a good time and learned a thing or two about procrastination. My hope is you'll be able to take action from the tips, strategies, and insights we've discussed.

Because that's the key right there — taking action.

You can read all the books in the world and learn fantastic ideas and tactics, but they won't create any meaningful change unless you apply them to your own life.

Unless you get your feet wet, nothing's going to change. Taking the leap from theory to practice, from knowing to doing, is what separates stagnation from growth and winners from dreamers.

Knowledge is intended for use — not applying it is a vain and foolish thing to do. I feel this message is more appropriate at the end of a book on procrastination than anywhere else.

Before the two of us part ways, I'd like to say thank you for reading my guide.

I'm aware that you could have chosen any other book on the subject of procrastination, and I'm thrilled you chose this one. So thanks for downloading my book and reading all the way to the end.

I'd love to hear your feedback. Please leave a review on Amazon if you like it!

Thanks so much!

Dr. Marybeth Crane is passionate about sharing with you her wellness series! Her goal is to help you attain a happy, healthy, stress-free life and make age just a number! Let her guide you from toxic behaviors to enlightened success using the tools she learned from conquering her own demons and poor habits!

Dr. Crane is a board-certified Podiatric foot and ankle surgeon who has been in private practice, specializing in sports medicine, for over 25 years. She successfully built a multi-million-dollar private practice from humble beginnings with her mother answering the phone. Dr. Crane now lectures around the country on business and practice management topics.

Dr. Crane has written several books on running injuries and authors a blog at www.myrundoc.com that is solely focused on sports medicine and running topics.

She also authors a blog on women's health and wellness issues as well as relationships, communication and the issues surrounding the lovely aging process at www.fitfiftyandfabulous.com.

Her main goal as a motivational speaker and author is to convince everyone that positive thinking is potent, exercise is the most powerful drug physicians can prescribe, and choosing a healthy lifestyle will help combat the lovely aging process. She can help you with the small and big changes that will assist you in changing your life for the better! The one percent changes daily are mighty!

In her spare time, she has been competitively running for more than 40 years. It definitely helps burn off the crazy! Dr. Crane has completed more than 20 marathons, a dozen or so Half-Ironman and 2 Full Ironman Triathlons. She is blessed with three wonderful daughters and two stepdaughters; so, she also has a boy dog! Her husband is truly a saint.

Contact her at marybeth@fitfiftyandfabulous.com. Follow her @myrundoc on Twitter, @fitfiftyandfabulous on Facebook, and @myrundoc.crane on Instagram.

We look forward to your questions and comments! If you liked this short read, check out her other books and please leave a review on Amazon!

www.ingramcontent.com/pod-product-compliance
Lightning Source LLC
Chambersburg PA
CBHW030526220526
45463CB00007B/2736